For SIE

For SIE

Red-breasted
pygmy parrot
(New Guinea)

Eclectus parrots
(New Guinea)

♂   ♀

Hyacinth macaw
(South America)

Published by Roaring Brook Press
Roaring Brook Press is a division of Holtzbrinck
Publishing Holdings Limited Partnership
120 Broadway, New York, NY 10271 • mackids.com

Copyright © 2021 by Maxwell Eaton III
All rights reserved

Library of Congress Cataloging-in-Publication Data is available.
ISBN 978-1-250-23255-7

Our books may be purchased in bulk for promotional, educational, or
business use. Please contact your local bookseller or the Macmillan
Corporate and Premium Sales Department at (800) 221-7945 ext.
5442 or by email at MacmillanSpecialMarkets@macmillan.com.

First edition, 2021 • Book design by Jennifer Browne
Printed in China by Toppan Leefung Printing Ltd.,
Dongguan City, Guangdong Province

1 3 5 7 9 10 8 6 4 2

Palm cockatoo
(New Guinea)

These are parrots.
There are about 350 different parrot species across the world.

PARROTS ARE FOUND MOSTLY IN TROPICAL AND SUBTROPICAL AREAS.

Many parrot species look wildly different, and yet they all share features that make you say, "That's a parrot."

Large heads
- House powerful beak muscles
- Large brains

Sharp, curved beaks
- For crushing seeds and tearing into fruit

Imperial Amazon (Dominica)

My surprised face.

Strong, flexible tongues
- For eating fruit, licking nectar, manipulating food, and vocalizing

Especially noticeable are parrots' colorful feathers, which help them find mates.

Rainbow lorikeet (SE Asia and Australia)

Of course, what looks flashy out in the open may help some parrots blend in, depending on the backdrop.
Great camouflage.
How can she see me?
Scaly-breasted lorikeet (Australia)
SOME PARROTS MAY BE MORE BEAUTIFUL THAN WE'LL EVER KNOW. PARROTS CAN SEE ULTRA-VIOLET LIGHT, WHICH, WHEN COMBINED WITH THE COLORS WE CAN SEE, MAY REVEAL FEATHER DISPLAYS BEYOND OUR IMAGINATION.
Actually, you get used to it.

Parrot couples can be affectionate, spending time cuddling and grooming each other. Many species even mate for life.

The kakapo of New Zealand may live one hundred years or longer! But they're unique among parrots in even more ways.

Most parrots spend their days eating some combination of seeds, nuts, fruits, berries, buds, or flowers. Many have their specialties.

HYACINTH MACAWS CRACK LARGE PALM NUTS WITH POWERFUL BEAKS.

BLUE-WINGED PARROTS FEED ON GRASS SEEDS.

One parrot has been known to eat even larger creatures. The Antipodes parakeet may enter the grassy burrow of a small seabird and finish its meal before leaving.

Trick-or-treat.

THIS SORT OF MEAT-EATING IS RARE AMONG PARROTS.

Oh, I do like my parrots rare.

Grey-backed storm petrel

One thing all parrots share is a keen mind with vocal learning abilities. Many can copy sounds. Most famously, human speech.

Eclectus parrot
(New Guinea)

Scientists believe that some wild groups of parrots may create their own languages using sounds that they make up or borrow.

These languages could be used to call each other by name, label objects, share where to find food, alert others to danger, and even pass information from one generation to the next.

Of course, it's no mystery that clever creatures like to play. Keas are known for wrestling, toying with objects, and even rolling pebbles down hills just for fun.

Are we taking it too far?

Kea (New Zealand)

The good news is that you can begin to help by learning more about our bright feathered friends and then teaching others.

Because parrots are wild animals.

PARROT FILE

Some parrot nest sites

Tree hollows
(most common site)
Thick-billed parrot

Burrows
Burrowing parrot
(naturally)

Stick nests
Monk parakeet

Termite mounds
Golden-shouldered
parrot

Rotten logs
Kakapo

Rock crevices
Abaco parrot

Most
sulphur-crested
cockatoos are
left-footed.

Eating clay

- Some parrots eat fruit that is toxic before it is ripe

- Eating clay may help these parrots pass the toxins out of their bodies

← Blue-headed parrots in Peru

Parrots lay 1 to 8 eggs depending on the species.

Chicks hatch at different times, in the order the eggs are laid.

Further Research

BOOKS FOR PARROTLETS

Alex the Parrot, Stephanie Spinner, illustrated by Meilo So, Alfred A. Knopf, 2012.

Parrots Over Puerto Rico, Susan L. Roth and Cindy Trumbore, illustrated by Susan L. Roth, Lee & Low Books, Inc., 2013.

BOOKS FOR KAKAPOS

Parrots: A Guide to the Parrots of the World, Tony Juniper and Mike Parr, Yale University Press, 1998.

Parrots of the Wild, Catherine A. Toft and Timothey F. Wright, University of California Press, 2015.